FIRST PICTURE
ATLAS

By Antony Mason

with maps by John Woodcock and Eugene Fleury

KINGFISHER
Larousse Kingfisher Chambers Inc.
95 Madison Avenue
New York, New York 10016

First American edition 1994
2 4 6 8 10 9 7 5 3 1
Copyright © Larousse plc

LIBRARY OF CONGRESS CATALOGING-IN-PUBLICATION DATA
Mason, Antony,
The Kingfisher first picture atlas / by Antony Mason : [John
Woodcock and Eugene Fleury, map illustrators]
p.   cm.
Includes index.
1. Children's atlases.   [1. Atlases.]   I. Woodcock, John, ill.
II. Fleury, Eugene, ill.   III. Title.
G1021.M253   1994   <G&M>
912–dc20   93-48655   CIP   MAP AC

ISBN 0–7534–5153–0
Printed in Italy

Editor: Catherine Headlam
Designers: John Jamieson and Terry Woodley
Consultant: Keith Lye
Additional research by Andrea Moran and Michael Butterworth
Map illustrations by Eugene Fleury (all political maps and the climate
map); John Woodcock (all picture maps)
Additional illustrations by Maggie Brand (Maggie Mundy Illustrators
Agency); Stephen Conlin; Jeremy Gower (B. L. Kearley Ltd.); Janos
Marffy (Kathy Jakeman Agency): Adam Marshall; Josephine Martin
(Garden Studio); Ralph Orme; Clare Roberts (Garden Studio);
Roger Stuart; Joanna Williams (B. L. Kearley Ltd.)

Contents

About this Atlas

Most of the world's land is divided up into seven large continents. In this atlas, six of the continents are shown twice. The first map shows all of the independent countries within each continent. [An independent country is one with its own government.] And the second map shows the major rivers, lakes, and mountains. The seventh continent, Antarctica, has just one map. This is because people don't live there all year round.

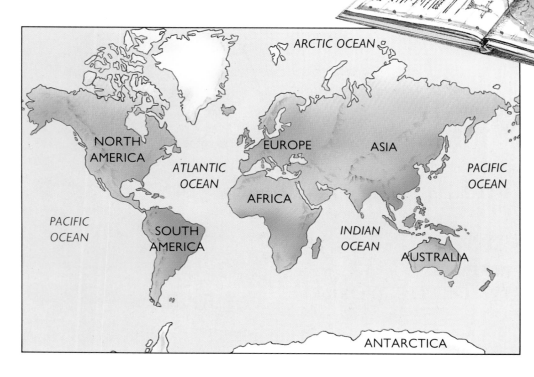

About the maps

On the first maps each country is clearly marked in a separate color with its capital city. The second maps are picture maps. They show the kind of animals that live on each continent, some of the plants that grow there, and the main industries. It is not possible, however, to show every spot where, for example, tigers or factories are found. There will be tigers and factories in other places besides those marked.

On the maps you will see where the biggest mountain ranges are, where the rivers flow to, what the names of the largest lakes are, as well as the names of the countries and their capital cities.

Each map has a scale. This will help you to work out how large the continent really is.

| 0 | 200 | 400 | 600 | 800 kilometers |
| 0 | 100 | 200 | 300 | 400 | 500 miles |

Hills and mountains

Country border

Capital city

Country

River

Important city

Where is it?

If you want to find a particular place in the atlas, look for it first in the index. After the place name you will see a page number and then a number and a letter, such as **4C**. This is the grid reference. Remember it as you turn to the page. Now look for the grid number (in a red circle) at the top and bottom of the page. There is a faint blue line running on either side of them, up and down the page. Now look for the letter, on the left- and right-hand sides of the page and the lines running beside these. You will find the place you are looking for in the square where the lines meet.

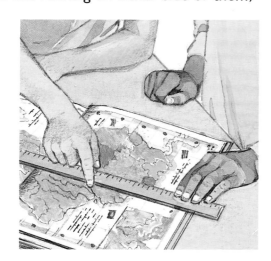

MAKING A MEAL OF IT

On the picture-map pages there is a box showing a typical meal from that continent, using the food that is grown there. Of course, people eat a huge variety of things in the different parts of any continent. None the less, each continent does have its own, individual kinds of food, and its own traditional recipes based on the common ingredients that are found in the region.

ANSWER THAT!

On all the map pages there is a box called "Answer That!" This asks you three questions about the map. You should be able to answer each of the questions by studying the map carefully. Look hard, and you are sure to find the solution—but some questions may require more looking than others! The correct answers to all the questions are given on page 38. Can you think of other questions to ask?

Where it comes from and where it is made

The picture maps include a series of symbols showing you the main products and industries of a region.

A factory marks an **industry** or industrial area, and logs marks the **lumber industry**. An oil rig shows where **oil** is drilled, and a flame shows **gas** production.

A mining wagon full of coal or metal, or two gemstones, show where **mining** takes place.

A beach umbrella and suitcase shows that the **tourist industry** is important in that area.

Large-scale **fishing** is represented by a trawler, and **animal farming** by a bull (for beef cattle), a dairy cow, a sheep, and a pig.

An ear of corn, a stalk of wheat, and a rice plant show where these important **cereals** are grown.

Various kinds of **fruit farming** are important in many parts of the world. These are shown by apples and pears, oranges and lemons, bananas, and grapes (which are also used to make wine).

Tea, coffee, and cocoa are important and valuable crops. These are shown by tea leaves, coffee beans, and cocoa pods.

Palm trees provide other crops such as copra from coconut palms (used to make coconut oil), dates from date palms, and palm oil.

Peanuts are sometimes known as groundnuts, and **sugar cane** is used to make sugar. Natural **rubber** is harvested from trees, and **cotton** comes from the fluffy seedheads of the cotton plant.

 Factory

 Lumber

 Oil

 Gas

 Mining

 Gemstones

 Tourism

 Fishing

 Beef cattle

 Dairy cows

 Sheep

 Pigs

 Corn

 Wheat

 Rice

 Apples and pears

 Citrus fruits

 Bananas

 Grapes and wine

 Tea

 Coffee

 Cocoa

 Palm tree

 Peanuts

 Sugar cane

 Rubber

 Cotton

How maps are made

Maps are very clear and simple pictures of the world, so that we can see where places are, and how we might get from one place to another. Maps of the world are the result of years of work by navigators and surveyors who have visited the places and measured the shapes of land, the heights of mountains, the courses of rivers, and the position of towns and cities. In recent years, pictures from space satellites have helped to make maps even more accurate.

One of the big problems with maps of the world is that the world is not flat, but round.

To draw a flat map of the round world we have to cheat a little. Imagine the world as an orange.

Peel the skin off the orange, into segments of equal sizes. See how the segments are oval-shaped?

With the whole peel removed you have a true picture of the surface of the world divided into a row of oval segments.

But this does not make a very helpful map. So we cheat by stretching the Earth's surface to fill in the gaps between the segments to make a rectangle.

Map and scales

1. Using scale is a way of drawing places very much smaller than they are in real life, but still showing exactly where they are. If you are in Paris you can see the Eiffel Tower at its real size.

2. A map of the area around the Eiffel Tower will need to be drawn smaller than real size—to a smaller scale. So, for example, every inch on the map is equal to 600 feet of the real place or area.

3. Maps can be drawn to any scale, depending on what they are trying to show. A map of Paris shows the area of the city and two sizes of roads, but cannot show the Eiffel Tower in detail.

4. With an even smaller scale, a map will show much less detail about the city itself, but more about the country around it. A map of France will simply show where Paris is placed in the country.

Make your own map

Try making your own map of a place you know well, such as the area between your home and your school. Imagine how it would look from above. Draw in the streets, and show where all the main buildings are. Add any railroads, parks, rivers, and bridges. Keep the map as simple as possible by using symbols so that you can get more information into a small space. Could your friends use the map to find your home?

Climate and land

Every part of the world has its own climate or pattern of weather. It may be warm in summer, rainy in spring, and very cold in winter. Or it may be hot all year round. The climate of a country depends on the shape of its land, as well as its position in the world.

	Polar
	Cool and snowy
	Temperate
	Dry land and desert
	Tropical
	Mountain

This map of the world shows where the six main types of climate are found. Each climate is shown in a different color.

A **temperate climate** has warm summers and cool winters, and plenty of rain, which is good for farming.

SOME WORLD FACTS

Longest river the Nile River (4,160 miles)
Highest mountain Mount Everest (29,028 feet)
Highest waterfall Angel Falls, Venezuela (3,212 feet)
Largest country Russia (6.5 million square miles)
Smallest independent country the Vatican City State, in Italy (109 acres)
Largest continent Asia
Smallest continent Australia
Largest ocean the Pacific

The world can be divided into two halves by an imaginary line called the equator. The tropics form a band around the equator between two more imaginary lines called the Tropic of Cancer and the Tropic of Capricorn. The tropics receive the heat of the Sun from directly overhead. A **tropical climate** is hot and there is plenty of rain.

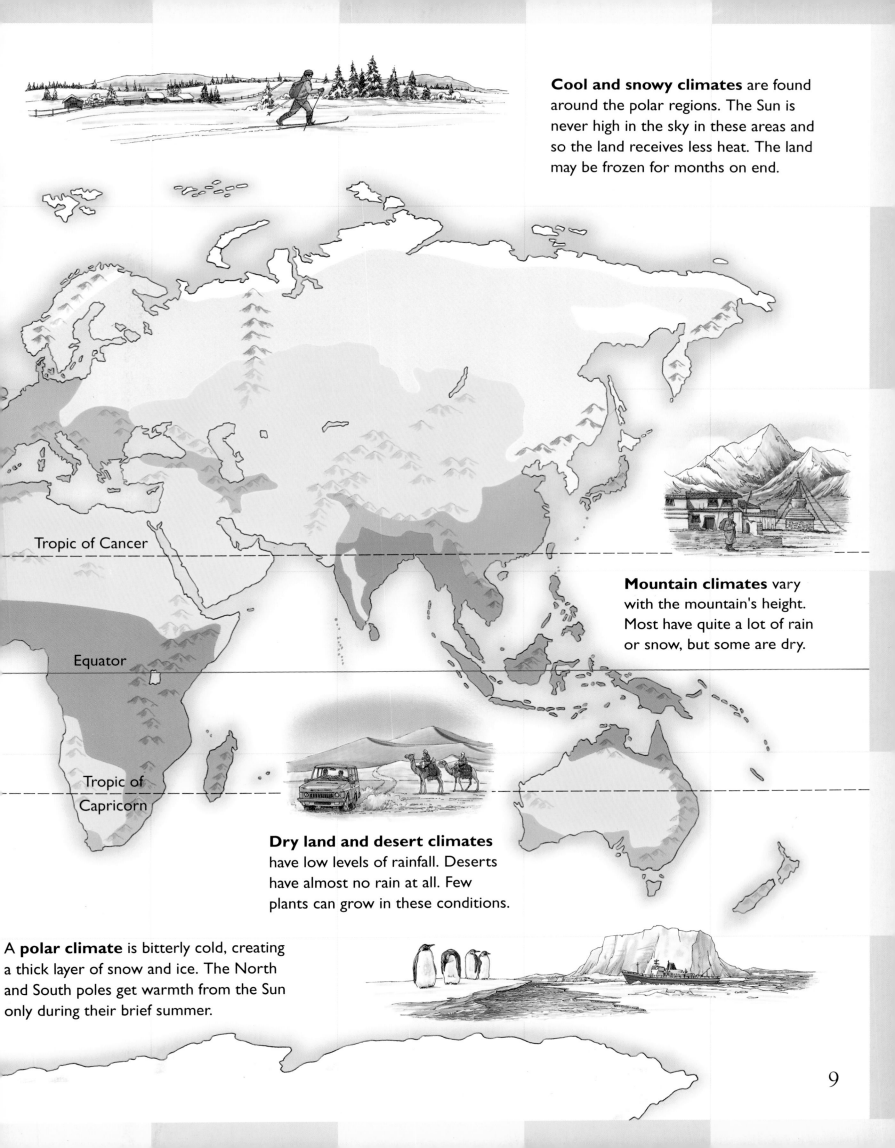

Cool and snowy climates are found around the polar regions. The Sun is never high in the sky in these areas and so the land receives less heat. The land may be frozen for months on end.

Tropic of Cancer

Equator

Tropic of Capricorn

Mountain climates vary with the mountain's height. Most have quite a lot of rain or snow, but some are dry.

Dry land and desert climates have low levels of rainfall. Deserts have almost no rain at all. Few plants can grow in these conditions.

A **polar climate** is bitterly cold, creating a thick layer of snow and ice. The North and South poles get warmth from the Sun only during their brief summer.

North America

Two English-speaking countries occupy most of North America: Canada and the United States of America. The third country, Mexico, is Spanish-speaking.

The United States is the world's richest and most powerful country. It is divided into 50 states.

To the south lies the warm Caribbean Sea, with hundreds of islands. A ribbon of land links North America to South America and contains a cluster of Spanish-speaking countries. Together these are known as Central America.

The Inuit (or Eskimo) people live in the very cold Arctic lands. In the past, they made houses called igloos from blocks of snow, and traveled on dogsleds. Now many live in towns and use motorized snowmobiles.

kilometers
0   400   800   1200   1600

miles
0   200   400   600   800   1000

Greenland is the largest island in the world. Although it is close to North America, its government is linked to Denmark. Most of the land is covered with snow and ice.

Greenland (Denmark)

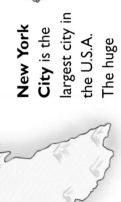

New York City is the largest city in the U.S.A. The huge Statue of Liberty stands on an island in New York Harbor.

St. Pierre et Miquelon (France)

HUDSON BAY

Alaska (U.S.A.)

Yukon River

Mackenzie River

C A N A D A

Saskatchewan River

Canada is the second largest country in the world. The northern part is remote and empty. Most people live in the south, close to the U.S.A.

ARCTIC OCEAN

ATLANTIC OCEAN

PACIFIC OCEAN

INDIAN OCEAN

The Hawaiian Islands lie about 2,360 miles (3,800 km) from the west coast of the U.S.A., in the Pacific Ocean. This group of islands forms the state of Hawaii. The islands are boxed to show that they are drawn closer to the mainland of the U.S.A. than they really are.

Hawaii (U.S.A.)

Washington D.C. is the capital of the U.S.A. It contains government buildings, such as the U.S. Capitol, where the U.S. Congress meets.

St. Kitts and Nevis are two small Caribbean islands, which together form the smallest independent country in North America.

For the capital cities of the smaller islands, look up the country name in the index.

The Panama Canal was opened in 1914. Before then, ships had to sail all the way around South America to travel between the Pacific and the Atlantic oceans.

Mexico is a Spanish-speaking country with volcanoes and mountains, and long, sandy beaches. Its capital, Mexico City, is one of the largest cities in the world.

ANSWER THAT!
1. Which country shares the southern border of the United States?
2. Which is the largest island in the Caribbean Sea?
3. Which island is called green, but is hardly green at all?

Map labels

UNITED STATES OF AMERICA

PACIFIC OCEAN

ATLANTIC OCEAN

San Francisco
Los Angeles
Snake River
Colorado River
Missouri River
Red River
Arkansas River
Rio Grande
Dallas
GREAT LAKES
L. Superior
L. Huron
L. Michigan
L. Ontario
L. Erie
Saint Lawrence
Montreal
Ottawa
Toronto
Boston
New York City
Detroit
Chicago
Philadelphia
Washington D.C.
Ohio River
Mississippi River

MEXICO
Monterrey
Guadalajara
Mexico City
GULF OF MEXICO

Bermuda (U.K.)

BAHAMAS
Nassau
Havana
C U B A
Cayman Islands (U.K.)
JAMAICA
Kingston
HAITI
Port-au-Prince
DOMINICAN REPUBLIC
Santo Domingo
Puerto Rico (U.S.A.)
San Juan
Virgin Islands (U.S.A./U.K.)
Anguilla (U.K.)
ST. KITTS AND NEVIS
ANTIGUA AND BARBUDA
Guadeloupe (France)
Martinique (France)
DOMINICA
Montserrat (U.K.)
ST. LUCIA
BARBADOS
ST. VINCENT AND THE GRENADINES
GRENADA
Netherlands Antilles (Neth.)
TRINIDAD AND TOBAGO
Port-of-Spain

CARIBBEAN SEA

GUATEMALA
Guatemala City
BELIZE
Belmopan
HONDURAS
Tegucigalpa
EL SALVADOR
San Salvador
NICARAGUA
Managua
COSTA RICA
San José
PANAMA
Panama City
Panama Canal

MAKING A MEAL OF IT

Every November Americans celebrate Thanksgiving by eating the traditional meal of turkey with cranberry sauce, sweet potatoes, and pumpkin pie.

Beavers live in many of the smaller rivers of North America. They cut down young trees to build dams and homes called lodges. The dams block the streams and create small lakes.

Lumber is one of the most important products of Canada. The wood is made into planks and paper. The workers who cut down the trees are called lumberjacks.

Mount McKinley, in Alaska, is the highest mountain in North America. It rises to 20,321 feet (6,194 m) It is surrounded by the Denali National Park. (Denali is the Native American name for Mount McKinley).

The Great Lakes lie on the border between Canada and the U.S.A. and are linked to the Atlantic by the St. Lawrence River.

GREENLAND

RUSSIA

Polar bear

Musk ox

Harp seal

Narwhal

Walrus

Ringed seal

Right whale

Snow goose

Puffin

Canada goose

HUDSON BAY

Beaver

Arctic wolf

Arctic hare

Caribou

Mackenzie River

Moose

Rocky Mountain goat

Saskatchewan River

Brown bear

ROCKY MOUNTAINS

Yukon River

MOUNT McKINLEY

Bald eagle

Salmon

The Mississippi and Missouri rivers together are about 3,730 miles (6,000 km) long—the longest river system in North America.

Corn has been grown in North America for thousands of years. It is eaten as a vegetable, and as popcorn or flour.

Lobster

Cape Canaveral

Hibiscus

Hummingbird

Helliconia

ANSWER THAT!

1. What is the name of the sea mammal with one long spiked tusk on its nose?

2. Which river forms part of the southern U.S. border?

3. Which "dog" is not a dog at all but lives in underground "towns?"

L. Superior
GREAT LAKES
L. Michigan
L. Huron
L. Erie
L. Ontario
Saint Lawrence River
Ohio River
APPALACHIAN MOUNTAINS

Black bear
Raccoon
Prairie dog
Skunk
Missouri River
Rattlesnake
Arkansas River
Bison
Kit fox
Red River
Coyote
Pelican
Mississippi River

Alligator
Coconuts
Rock beauty

GULF OF MEXICO
Cuban hogfish

GRAND CANYON
Colorado River
Snake River
Monarch butterfly
Saguaro cactus
Gila monster
Rio Grande
Quetzal

Swordfish
Dolphin
Gray whale
Humpback whale

Sugar cane is grown in Central America, and on many Caribbean islands. The tall, thick stems are crushed to extract the clear, sweet juice, which is then made into sugar.

The Grand Canyon in Arizona is one of the great natural wonders of the world. It was created by the Colorado River, which has cut a narrow gorge through the rock. In some places it is nearly a mile (1.6 km) deep.

Sequoias growing in California are the largest trees in the world. The tallest is a giant sequoia that has grown to over 360 feet (110 m). Some sequoias are believed to be nearly 3,000 years old.

13

Surinam is the smallest independent country in South America. It was governed by the Netherlands until 1975.

French Guiana (or Guyane) is governed by France. European rockets are launched from its space station at Kourou (see page 16).

Brazil is by far the largest country in South America. Much of the land area is taken up by the basin of the Amazon River. Brazil is rich in iron, and produces more coffee than any other country.

Ecuador means equator in Spanish. Although the coasts are hot, the center of the country is high in the Andes, where the weather is cooler.

Equator

ARCTIC OCEAN

ATLANTIC OCEAN

PACIFIC OCEAN

INDIAN OCEAN

CARIBBEAN SEA

VENEZUELA

Caracas ■

COLOMBIA

Bogotá ■

Orinoco River

GUYANA

Georgetown ■

SURINAM

Paramaribo ■

FRENCH GUIANA

Cayenne ■

ECUADOR

Quito ■

PERU

Lima ■

Machu
Picchu ●

BOLIVIA

La Paz ■

ANDES MOUNTAINS

Marañón River

Ucayali River

Japurá River

Rio Negro

Amazon River

Madeira River

Xingu River

Tocantins River

São Francisco River

Paraguay River

BRAZIL

Brasília ■

PACIFIC OCEAN

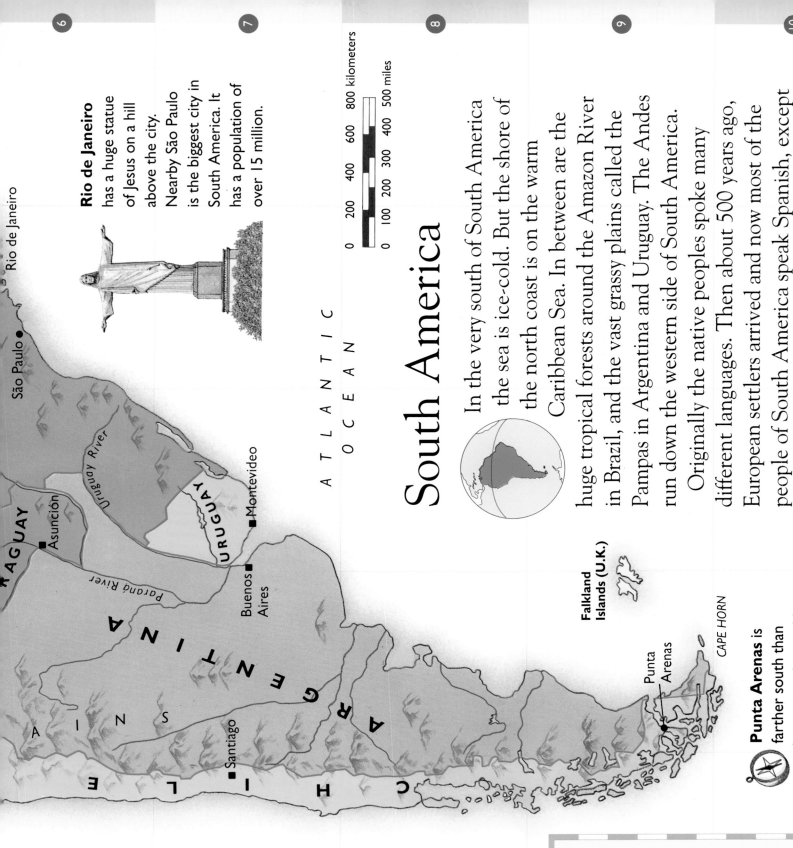

South America

In the very south of South America the sea is ice-cold. But the shore of the north coast is on the warm Caribbean Sea. In between are the huge tropical forests around the Amazon River in Brazil, and the vast grassy plains called the Pampas in Argentina and Uruguay. The Andes run down the western side of South America. Originally the native peoples spoke many different languages. Then about 500 years ago, European settlers arrived and now most of the people of South America speak Spanish, except in Brazil, where the main language is Portuguese.

Rio de Janeiro has a huge statue of Jesus on a hill above the city. Nearby São Paulo is the biggest city in South America. It has a population of over 15 million.

ATLANTIC OCEAN

Rio de Janeiro

São Paulo

URUGUAY

Montevideo

Uruguay River

Asunción

Paraná River

ARGENTINA

Buenos Aires

Santiago

CHILE

ANDES

Falkland Islands (U.K.)

Punta Arenas

CAPE HORN

Punta Arenas is farther south than any other city in the world.

| 0 | 200 | 400 | 600 | 800 kilometers |
| 0 | 100 | 200 | 300 | 400 | 500 miles |

La Paz is the world's highest capital city, standing 11,900 feet (3,627 m) above sea level. The air is thin at this height, and visitors from other lower countries can feel quite breathless.

Machu Picchu is a ruined city of the ancient Inca people. It lies high in the mountains of Peru and remained hidden for hundreds of years before it was rediscovered in 1911.

ANSWER THAT!

1. How many countries in South America begin with the letter B?
2. What is the name of the longest and thinnest country in South America?
3. Which country has coasts on the Pacific Ocean and on the Caribbean Sea?

ANSWER THAT!

1. Which South American animal likes to hang upside down from branches?

2. One animal likes to eat ants, which it picks up with its sticky tongue. What is its name?

3. Which frog can be used to make poison arrows?

Cocoa is grown in the warm parts of South America. Chocolate is made from the seeds, or beans, that are found inside the cocoa pods.

The Amazon River is 4,007 miles (6,448 km) long (slightly shorter than the Nile River in Africa). However, it carries far more water than any other river in the world, and 60 times more than the Nile.

The Angel Falls is the highest waterfall in the world. The water tumbles from a height of 3,212 feet (979 m).

Lake Titicaca is the largest freshwater lake in South America. It is 12,506 feet (3,812 m) above sea level. The ferry service across the lake is the world's highest

CARIBBEAN SEA

PACIFIC OCEAN

A N D E S

GUIANA HIGHLANDS

Orinoco River

Rio Negro

Japurá River

Marañón River

Ucayali River

Madeira River

Amazon River

Xingu River

Tocantins River

São Francisco River

Kourou

Surinam road

Giant leatherback turtle

Macaw

ANGEL FALLS

Howler monkey

Kapok tree

Harpy eagle

Brazil nut tree

Anaconda

Poison arrow frog

Llama

LAKE TITICACA

Spider monkey

Capybara

Sloth

Piranha

Manatee

Marmoset

Tarantula

Toucan

Kinkajou

Hummingbird

Giant anteater

Tapir

The Atacama Desert is one of the driest places on Earth. Some parts of it have gone 400 years without rain.

Condors are large vultures that live in the Andes. Some have a wingspan of over 10 feet (3 m). They feed on the bodies of dead animals.

The Andes form the longest mountain range in the world. They stretch for 4,500 miles (7,250 km). The highest peak is Aconcagua, which rises to 22,830 feet (6,959 m).

Soccer is a favorite sport all over South America. Brazil was the first country to win the World Cup three times.

The Pampas covers much of Argentina and Uruguay. Large herds of beef cattle are raised on these huge grassy plains. They are looked after by cowboys called gauchos.

ATLANTIC OCEAN

Elephant seals are the largest of all seals. They live in cold waters and breed on the shores of southern Argentina. Male elephant seals can be as much as 20 feet (6 m) long.

MAKING A MEAL OF IT

Many of our common foods come originally from Central and South America. These include corn, tomatoes, and potatoes. A common meal in South America consists of beef with boiled rice or potatoes, tomatoes, and slices of fried plantain (a fruit like a banana).

Jaguar

Uruguay River

Paraná River

Guinea pig

Rhea

Vicuña

ACONCAGUA

ATACAMA DESERT

Chinchilla

Monkey puzzle tree

Armadillo

Patagonian hare

Elephant seal

Fur seal

CAPE HORN

Blue whale

Magellan penguin

17

Europe

There are more than 40 countries in Europe, and about as many languages. This is a wealthy part of the world with many old, historic cities and lots of big industries producing cars, chemicals, medicines, and other products. It generally has mild weather, with plenty of rain, which is good for farming. Southern Europe, around the Mediterranean Sea, has very warm summers, while the north is cooler with long, cold, and dark winters.

For the capital cities of the smallest countries, look up the country name in the index.

Brussels is the capital of Belgium. It is also the headquarters of the European Union (or EU). It has 12 member nations: Belgium, Denmark, France, Germany, Greece, Ireland, Italy, Luxembourg, the Netherlands, Portugal, Spain, and the United Kingdom.

Paris is the capital of France and one of the largest cities in Europe. Its many famous buildings include the Eiffel Tower, a huge metal tower built in 1889.

| 0 | 200 | 400 | 600 | 800 kilometers |
| 0 | 100 | 200 | 300 | 400 | 500 miles |

The Vatican City State is the smallest country in the world. It lies inside the city of Rome. The Vatican is the headquarters of the Roman Catholic Church, which is led by the Pope.

Map labels

Reykjavik
ICELAND

Faeroe Islands
(Denmark)

ATLANTIC OCEAN

NORTH S

REPUBLIC OF IRELAND
Dublin
IRISH SEA
UNITED KINGDOM
London
ENGLISH CHANNEL
NETHERLANDS
Amster
Rhine Ri
BELGIUM
Brussels
LUXEMBOURG
Paris
Luxembo
Loire River
BAY OF BISCAY
F R A N C E
SWITZERLA
Rhône River
Po Ri
ANDORRA
MONACO
S P A I N
Ebro River
Madrid
Barcelona
Cors
(Fran
P O R T U G A L
Tajo River
Lisbon
Sardi
(Italy
Strait of Gibraltar
Gibraltar
(U.K.)
MEDITERRANEAN SEA

ARCTIC OCEAN
ATLANTIC OCEAN
PACIFIC OCEAN
INDIAN OCEAN

NORWEGIAN SEA

NORWAY

SWEDEN

FINLAND

RUSSIA

N. Dvina River

• Oslo

• Helsinki   • St. Petersburg

• Stockholm   • Tallinn

ESTONIA

BALTIC SEA

Riga ■   LATVIA

LITHUANIA

Vilnius •

• Minsk

■ Moscow

Ural River

NMARK
• Copenhagen

Kaliningrad
(Russia)

B E L A R U S

Don River

Berlin ■

P O L A N D

Warsaw ■

GERMANY

Volga River

Prague ■

CZECH REPUBLIC

River

SLOVAKIA

U K R A I N E

Vienna ■   ■ Bratislava

AUSTRIA

Budapest •

• Kiev

HTENSTEIN

HUNGARY

MOLDOVA

Dnepr
River

CASPIAN SEA

jubljana ■

■ Zagreb

R O M A N I A

Chisinau •

OVENIA

CROATIA

YUGOSLAVIA

SAN MARINO

Sarajevo •

• Belgrade

• Bucharest

BLACK SEA

me

BOSNIA-
HERZEGOVINA

BULGARIA

• Sofia

TICAN
Y STATE

Tirana •

Skopje •

Istanbul •

Istanbul is the largest
city in Turkey. Most
of Turkey is in Asia, but a
small part of it is in Europe.
Istanbul lies in both Europe
and Asia.

ALBANIA

GREECE

cily (Italy)

MACEDONIA

• Athens

TURKEY

• Valletta

MALTA

Crete (Greece)

Moscow is the capital of
Russia, and one of the
largest cities in Europe.
St. Basil's Cathedral is so
colorful that it looks as
though it might be made of
candy—but it is not!

ANSWER THAT!
1. Which country earned
its name because it is so
icy? (Clue: it is an island).
2. Which city in which
country is in both Europe
and Asia?
3. Which country in
Europe begins with the
letter C, but does not have
any sea around its borders?

19

MAKING A MEAL OF IT

One of the most famous dishes of Europe is pasta from Italy. Pasta is made of wheat flour. Spaghetti and ravioli are types of pasta. Ravioli consists of small pasta envelopes filled with meat or cheese. It is often eaten with a tomato sauce, and sprinkled with grated Parmesan cheese.

Cork comes from the thick bark of trees called cork oaks. Portugal is the world's largest producer of cork. Much of it is used to make corks for wine bottles.

Great Britain is the largest island in Europe. Other countries this far north have cold climates, but Britain is kept warm by the Gulf Stream, the warm ocean current from the Gulf of Mexico.

Wild boars are a kind of wild pig. They are found in many countries of Europe, including Spain and Germany.

Arctic tern

Sperm whale

Icelandic pony

Puffin

European

Lynx

Red deer

Salmon

Wolverine

KJOLEN MOUNTAINS

NORTH SEA

Cormorant

BALTIC S

Shamrock

Sole

Elbe River

Barn owl

Badger

Red squirrel

Rabbit

Lobster

Rhine River

Hedgehog

Loire River

Fox

ATLANTIC OCEAN

Chamois

Ibex

Marmot

Golden eagle

Lammergeier

Rhône River

Po River

ALPS

White stork

Tajo River

Ebro River

PYRENEES

CORSICA

Sardine

Barbary ape

SARDINIA

SICILY

MEDITERRANEAN

URAL MOUNTAINS

Gray seal

Polar bear

Reindeer

Wolf

Ptarmigan

N. Dvina River

Brown bear

Jay

Trout

Demoiselle crane

Weasel

Don River

Steppe eagle

Dnepr River

Pelican

Volga River

Suslik

Sturgeon

Rose

CARPATHIAN MOUNTAINS

Danube River

MOUNT ELBRUS ▲

BLACK SEA

CAUCASUS MOUNTAINS

CASPIAN SEA

Ural River

Squid

CRETE

ANSWER THAT!
1. A big fish-eating bird beginning with the letter P lives around the Black Sea. What is its name?
2. Where do you need to watch out for wolves and bears?
3. Where can you find a mountain goat-antelope beginning with the letter C?

The Volga River is the longest river in Europe. It flows 2,194 miles (3,531 km) through Russia to the Caspian Sea.

The Caspian Sea is a salt-water lake—the largest lake in the world. There, fish called sturgeon produce the eggs we know as caviar, one of the world's most expensive foods.

Bread is an important food and comes in many different varieties in Europe. It is usually made from wheat or rye flour. The bubbles in the bread come from adding yeast, which makes the dough rise.

Mount Elbrus is the highest mountain in Europe, rising to 18,510 feet (5,642 m). It is part of the Caucasus range, very close to Asia.

A
B
C
D
E
F

21

ARCTIC OCEAN

ATLANTIC OCEAN

PACIFIC OCEAN

INDIAN OCEAN

A R C T I

Russia is the largest country in the world. About one fifth of it lies in Europe, and the rest is in Asia.

■ Moscow

R U S S I A

Ob River

Yenisey River

Irtysh River

● Yekaterinburg

● Novosibirsk

M O

Mecca, in Saudi Arabia, is the most holy city of the Muslims. This is where the Prophet Muhammad was born. Every year over 500,000 pilgrims from around the world visit Mecca's main mosque.

T U R K E Y
Ankara ■
GEORGIA

CYPRUS
Nicosia ■   Tbilisi ■   **ARMENIA**
LEBANON
Beirut ■   Yerevan ●
Jerusalem ■   **SYRIA**   ■ Baku
■ Damascus   **AZERBAIJAN**   **TURKMENISTAN**
ISRAEL
JORDAN   Amman ■   Baghdad ■   Tehran ■   Ashgabat ■

K A Z A K H S T A N

UZBEKISTAN

Toshkent ■   **KYRGYZSTAN**   ● Almaty
Bishkek ■
Dushanbe ■
TAJIKISTAN

C H I N

Tigris River

S A U D I
Kuwait ■
City
KUWAIT
Mecca ●   **BAHRAIN**
Riyadh ■   **QATAR**
■ Doha
Abu Dhabi ■

I R A Q

I R A N

AFGHANISTAN   Kabul ■
Islamabad ■

P A K I S T A N

Indus River

RED SEA

A R A B I A

San'a ●   **UNITED ARAB EMIRATES**

Y E M E N   O M A N   ■ Muscat

Karachi ■   New Delhi ■   **NEPAL**   Kathmandu ■
Thimphu ■

ARABIAN SEA

Brahmaputra River

Salw
Riv

Asia

Asia is by far the largest of the seven continents. It stretches from the warm seas around the equator to the Arctic Circle, and includes hot deserts, freezing cold wastelands, and the Himalayas, the highest mountains in the world. China and India both have huge populations. Most of the people live around the edge of the continent, and much of the center and north is remote and empty. Although Asia has many poor people, it also includes some of the world's richest countries.

I N D I A

Ganges River   Dhaka ■
Calcutta ●
Godavari River

Bombay ●

BHUTAN
BANGLADESH

B U R M A
(M Y A N M A
Irrowad

Madras ●

BAY OF BENGAL

Rangoon (Yangon) ■

MALDIVES   **SRI LANKA**
■ Colombo

Andaman Islands (India)

● Malé

I N D I A N   O C E A N

The Maldives are a group of about 2,000 islands. Together they form the smallest country in Asia. It is also the world's flattest country.

Aleutian Islands (U.S.A.)

BERING SEA

The Trans-Siberian Railroad is the longest in the world. The 8-day journey from Moscow to Vladivostok covers over 5,000 miles (9,000 km).

Japan is made up of four main islands. Its capital, Tokyo, is among the biggest cities in the world. Japan produces cars, computers, toys, and many other products, which have made it one of the world's leading industrial nations.

Hong Kong is a tiny British territory on the coast of southern China. It is one of the world's great business centers with a very busy port. In 1997 Hong Kong will become part of China again.

China has a population of over a billion people. Most of them live in the eastern part of the country, where there are many big cities and good farmland.

ANSWER THAT!
1. What is the largest country in Asia (and also the largest country in the world)?
2. What is the capital of India?
3. Which country in Southeast Asia was named after King Philip II of Spain?

Lena River

Amur River

OCEAN

EAN

L. BAIKAL

OLIA

Ulan Bator

Harbin

Vladivostok

NORTH KOREA

Pyongyang

Beijing

SEA OF JAPAN

Seoul

SOUTH KOREA

Tokyo

J A P A N

PACIFIC OCEAN

ng He River

Shanghai

EAST CHINA SEA

ngtze (Chang Jiang) River

Wuhan

Chonqing

Guangzhou

Taipei

TAIWAN

Hong Kong (U.K.)

Macao (Portugal)

Hanoi

tiane

LAOS

V I E T N A M

ND

ngkok

MBODIA

hnom enh

SOUTH CHINA SEA

P H I L I P P I N E S

Manila

BRUNEI

Bandar Seri Begawan

MALAYSIA

Kuala Lumpur

SINGAPORE

IRIAN JAYA

I N D O N E S I A

Equator

Jakarta

23

ARCT

Polar bear

Lemming

Siberia is a huge, cold region that covers most of Asian Russia. There are mountains and forests, and vast frozen wastes—and very few people.

Reindeer

URAL MOUNTAINS

Ob River

Yeni... River

ANSWER THAT!

1. What is the correct name for a camel with two humps?
2. In which country can you find tigers?
3. Most rhinoceroses live in Africa, but there are small numbers in Asia as well. Where might you find one?

Saiga antelope

Irtysh River

ALTAI MOUNTAIN

The Arabian Peninsula is almost entirely hot, dry desert. Most of the peninsula is occupied by Saudi Arabia, which has no rivers at all.

Cedar of Lebanon

Sturgeon

Demoiselle crane

ARAL SEA

CASPIAN SEA

Goat

Euphrates River

Tigris River

Bactrian cam

Yak

RED SEA

Oryx

ARABIAN PENINSULA

Onager

Oil is one of the main products of the Middle East, the southwestern part of Asia. The oil comes from wells under the ground. It is made into gasoline and other products, such as Tarmac and plastics.

Camel

Dates

Indus River

Lammergeier

MOUNT EVEREST

HIMALAYAS

Tiger

ARABIAN SEA

Mount Everest, in the Himalayas, rises to 29,028 feet (8,848 m) and is the highest mountain in the world. It was first climbed in 1953. All ten of the world's highest mountains are in the Himalayas.

Indian elephant

BAY OF BENGAL

Cobra

INDIAN OCEAN

Orangu

OCEAN

Walrus

Harp seal

BERING SEA

armigan

Barnacle goose

Wolf

Lena River

IBERIA

Brown bear

Lake Baikal seal

Wild horse

LAKE BAIKAL

Amur River

SEA OF JAPAN

Great Wall of China

Japanese macaque

ERT

Huang He River

Crane

EAST CHINA SEA

Yangtze River (Chang Jiang)

Giant panda

PACIFIC OCEAN

Squid

Orchid

SOUTH CHINA SEA

Philippine eagle

Shrimp

Hornbill

Bird of paradise

SUMATRA

BORNEO

Komodo dragon

JAVA

Javanese rhinoceros

Tea is made from young leaves picked from tea bushes. It was grown in China for many years before it was taken to other countries.

The Gobi Desert is a huge wasteland in northern China. It can be very hot in summer, and bitterly cold in winter.

MAKING A MEAL OF IT

The food of southern Asia is famous for its spicy flavors. Spices include ginger, cumin, coriander, cinnamon, pepper, yellow turmeric, and hot red chilies. The Indian dish called lamb korma is cooked with yogurt and contains all these spices. It can be served with rice or bread.

Giant pandas are found in the forests of southern China. Bamboo is their main food. Although they are a protected species, there are very few pandas still living in the wild.

The Yangtze River (or Chang Jiang) in China is the longest river in Asia at 3,964 miles (6,380 km) long—and the third longest in the world (after the Nile and Amazon).

Rice is the most important food of South and East Asia. The rice plant is a kind of grass. It is usually grown in flooded fields, called paddies.

A B C D E F

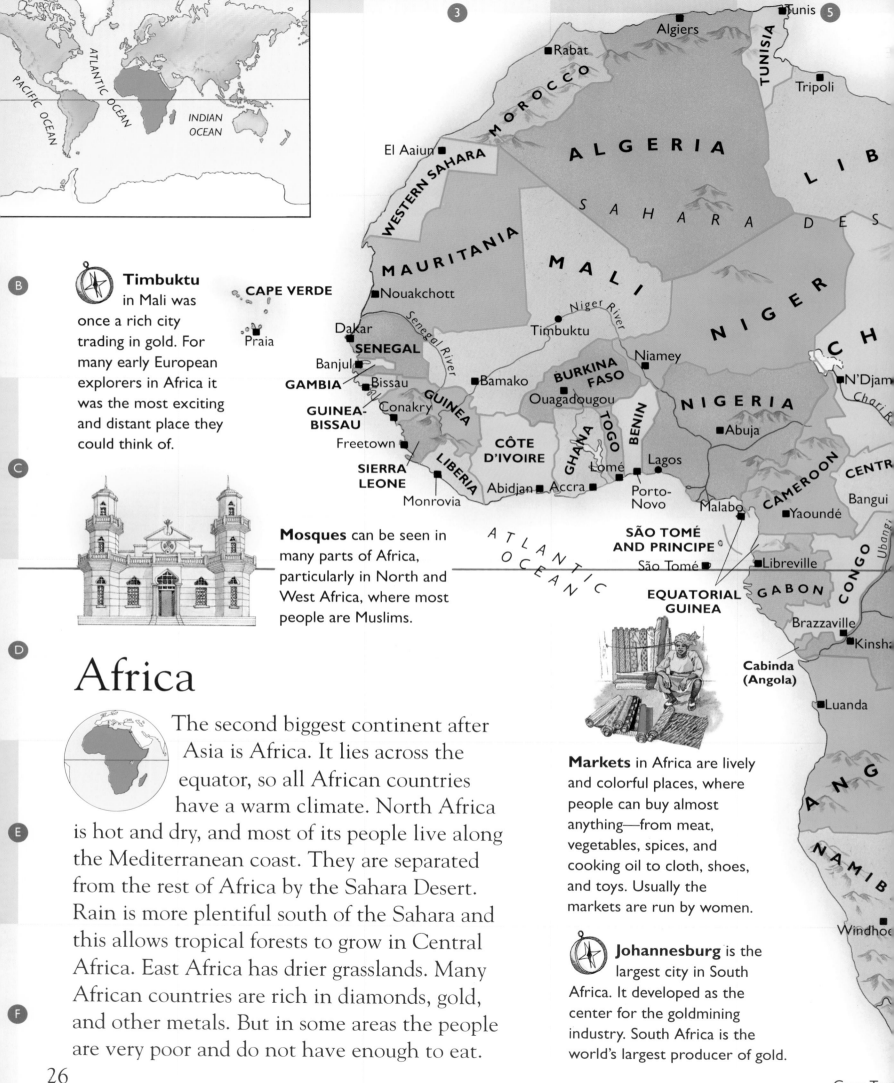

Timbuktu in Mali was once a rich city trading in gold. For many early European explorers in Africa it was the most exciting and distant place they could think of.

Mosques can be seen in many parts of Africa, particularly in North and West Africa, where most people are Muslims.

Africa

The second biggest continent after Asia is Africa. It lies across the equator, so all African countries have a warm climate. North Africa is hot and dry, and most of its people live along the Mediterranean coast. They are separated from the rest of Africa by the Sahara Desert. Rain is more plentiful south of the Sahara and this allows tropical forests to grow in Central Africa. East Africa has drier grasslands. Many African countries are rich in diamonds, gold, and other metals. But in some areas the people are very poor and do not have enough to eat.

Markets in Africa are lively and colorful places, where people can buy almost anything—from meat, vegetables, spices, and cooking oil to cloth, shoes, and toys. Usually the markets are run by women.

Johannesburg is the largest city in South Africa. It developed as the center for the goldmining industry. South Africa is the world's largest producer of gold.

Map labels

MOROCCO
Rabat
El Aaiun
WESTERN SAHARA
Algiers
TUNISIA
Tunis
Tripoli
LIB
ALGERIA
SAHARA
DES
MAURITANIA
Nouakchott
CAPE VERDE
Praia
Dakar
SENEGAL
Banjul
GAMBIA
Bissau
GUINEA-BISSAU
Conakry
GUINEA
Freetown
SIERRA LEONE
Monrovia
LIBERIA
CÔTE D'IVOIRE
Abidjan
Accra
GHANA
TOGO
Lomé
BENIN
Porto-Novo
MALI
Bamako
Timbuktu
Niger River
Senegal River
BURKINA FASO
Ouagadougou
Niamey
NIGER
CH
N'Djam
Chari
NIGERIA
Abuja
Lagos
Malabo
EQUATORIAL GUINEA
SÃO TOMÉ AND PRINCIPE
São Tomé
CAMEROON
Yaoundé
CENTR
Bangui
Ubang
GABON
Libreville
CONGO
Brazzaville
Kinsha
Cabinda (Angola)
Luanda
ANG
NAMIB
Windhoe
ATLANTIC OCEAN
PACIFIC OCEAN
ATLANTIC OCEAN
INDIAN OCEAN

26

MEDITERRANEAN SEA

Alexandria ■ Cairo

EGYPT

Nile River

RED SEA

SUDAN

Khartoum ■

Blue Nile River
White Nile River

Asmera ■

ERITREA

DJIBOUTI
Djibouti ■

ETHIOPIA

Addis Ababa ■

Shabelle River

SOMALIA

AFRICAN
PUBLIC

UGANDA

Kampala ■

KENYA

Mogadishu ■

ire River

RWANDA
Kigali ■
■ Nairobi

BURUNDI
Bujumbura ■

INDIAN OCEAN

Equator

SEYCHELLES
Victoria ■

Dodoma ■

TANZANIA

Dar es Salaam ■

IRE

MALAWI

COMOROS
Moroni ■
Mayotte
(France)

A

ZAMBIA

Lilongwe ■

MOZAMBIQUE

Lusaka ■

Zambezi River

MADAGASCAR

Antananarivo ■

MAURITIUS
Port Louis ■

Harare ■

ZIMBABWE

TSWANA

Limpopo River

Réunion
(France)

borone ■

Pretoria ■

Maputo ■

Johannesburg ■

SWAZILAND
Mbabane ■

nge

LESOTHO
Maseru ■

OUTH
FRICA

Cairo is the capital of Egypt. It has a population of over 7 million, making it easily the largest city in Africa. The Nile River flows through the city.

The pyramids lie just outside Cairo. They were built as giant tombs for the Egyptian kings over four thousand years ago. They are guarded by a stone Sphinx —half human, half lion.

Sudan is the largest country in Africa. The White Nile flows through the length of the country. The capital, Khartoum, lies at the place where the White Nile and the Blue Nile meet to become the Nile River.

The Seychelles is a group of about 100 islands off the east coast of Africa. This is the smallest country in the region. The islands are famous for their beautiful beaches of white sand.

ANSWER THAT!

1. Since 1992 Nigeria has had a new capital. What is the capital called?
2. Three countries in Africa begin with the letter Z. Can you name all of them?
3. What is the name of the country that lies inside the borders of Senegal?

kilometers
0   400   800   1200   1600

0   200   400   600   800   1000
miles

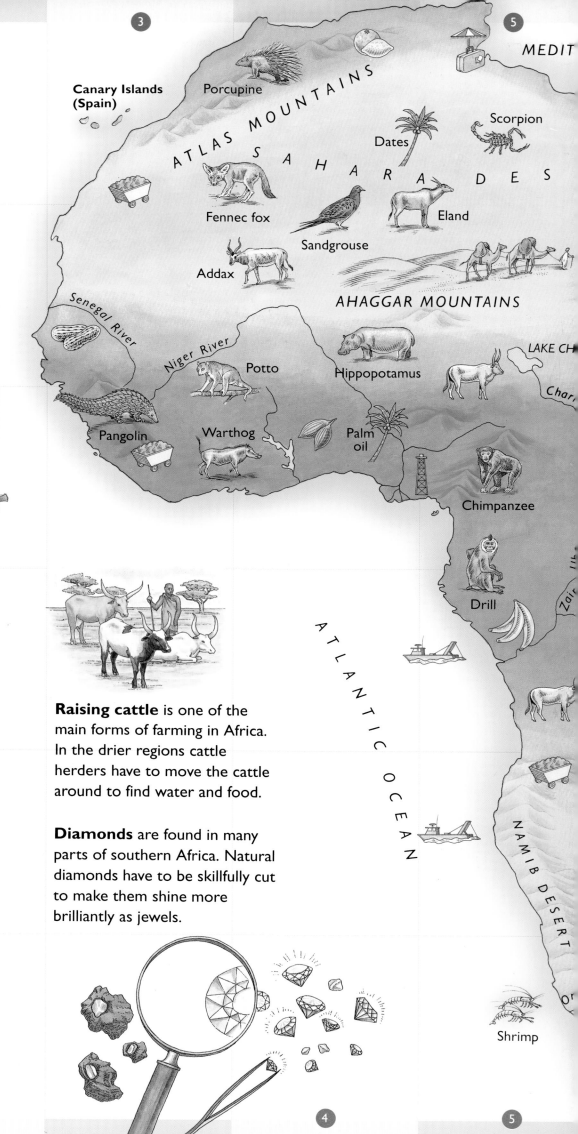

MAKING A MEAL OF IT

African cooking varies from region to region. In North Africa, the most famous dish is couscous—fluffy grains of steamed wheat. In West Africa, meat stews are often cooked with a spiced peanut sauce containing dried shrimps. (In Africa, peanuts are often called groundnuts.) The stews are eaten with sliced root vegetables, such as yams.

The Sahara Desert is the largest desert in the world. Much of it is covered by huge sand dunes, but in some areas there are high, rocky mountains. Camels are used to carry goods and people in desert areas.

ANSWER THAT!

1. What is the name of the lizard from Madagascar that can change color to match its background?
2. If you wanted to cross the Sahara Desert, what animal would you take to carry your baggage?
3. Which animal's name begins with two A's?

Raising cattle is one of the main forms of farming in Africa. In the drier regions cattle herders have to move the cattle around to find water and food.

Diamonds are found in many parts of southern Africa. Natural diamonds have to be skillfully cut to make them shine more brilliantly as jewels.

Canary Islands (Spain)

Porcupine

ATLAS MOUNTAINS

S A H A R A   D E S

Dates

Scorpion

Fennec fox

Sandgrouse

Eland

Addax

AHAGGAR MOUNTAINS

Senegal River

Niger River

Potto

Hippopotamus

LAKE CH

Char

Pangolin

Warthog

Palm oil

Chimpanzee

Drill

Zair

MEDIT

ATLANTIC OCEAN

NAMIB DESERT

Shrimp

28

EAN SEA

Coffee is made from the seeds of the coffee plant. It was probably first grown in Ethiopia.

Camel

Oryx

RED SEA

The Nile River is the longest river in the world. It flows 4,145 miles (6,670 km) from its source at Lake Victoria to the Mediterranean Sea.

oa

Leopard

Blue Nile River

Nile River

Hornbill

White Nile River

Acacia tree

Nubian goat

Aardvark

Cheetah

Shabelle River

rilla

Lion

The African elephant is the largest living animal on land. Elephants can grow to over 10 feet (3 m) tall and weigh 6 tons. Some elephants live to over 70 years of age.

LAKE VICTORIA

LAKE TANGANYIKA

MOUNT KILIMANJARO

Lake Victoria is the largest lake in Africa, and the third largest lake in the world. It lies between three countries: Kenya, Tanzania, and Uganda.

Giraffe

pi

LAKE MALAWI

Mount Kilimanjaro in Tanzania is the highest mountain in Africa. Its tallest peak rises to 19,340 feet (5,895 m) and is covered with snow throughout the year.

Zebra

rkats

Hyena

Gemsbok

MADAGASCAR

ich

Zambezi River

Chameleon

Hartebeest

Ring-tailed lemur

INDIAN OCEAN

Limpopo River

HARI ERT

Madagascar is the largest island off Africa. Some of its wildlife is found only in Madagascar—such as the ring-tailed lemur, a relative of the monkey family.

r

Wildebeest

Whale

Cape baboon

A

B

C

D

E

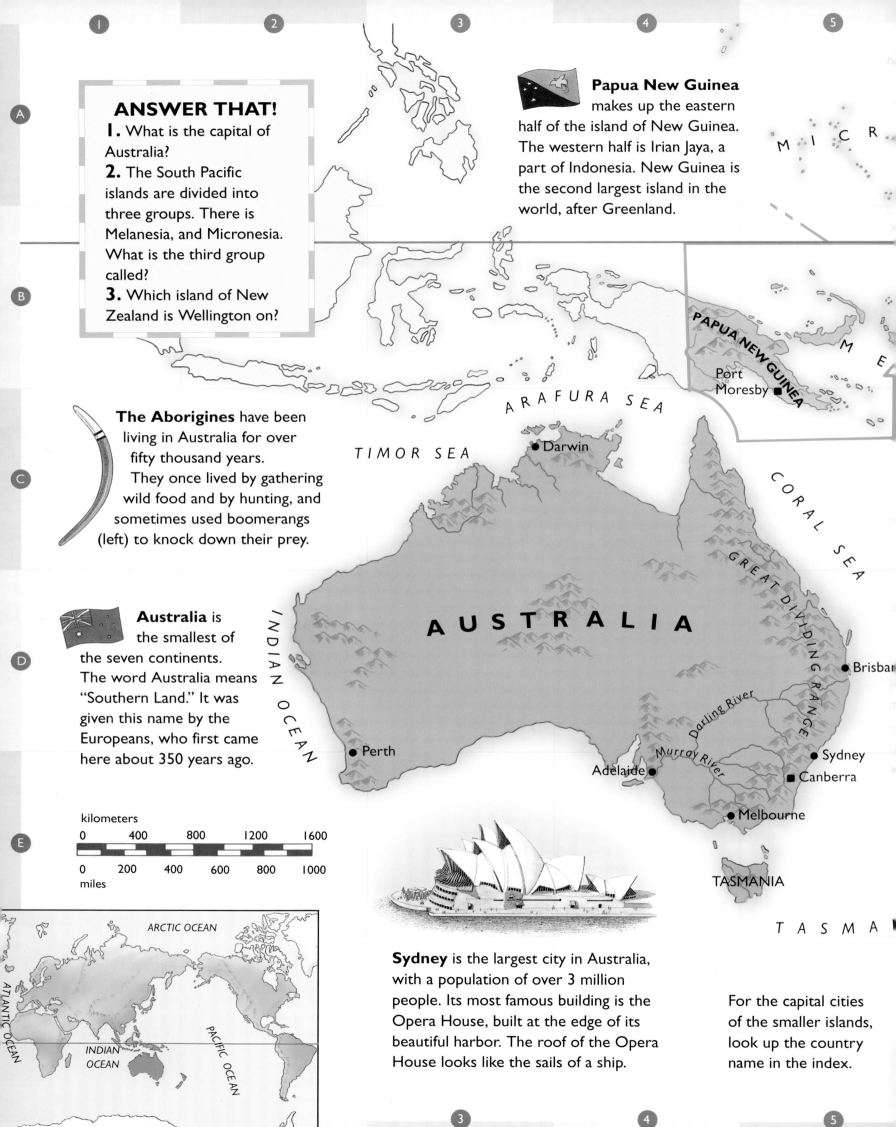

ANSWER THAT!
1. What is the capital of Australia?
2. The South Pacific islands are divided into three groups. There is Melanesia, and Micronesia. What is the third group called?
3. Which island of New Zealand is Wellington on?

Papua New Guinea makes up the eastern half of the island of New Guinea. The western half is Irian Jaya, a part of Indonesia. New Guinea is the second largest island in the world, after Greenland.

The Aborigines have been living in Australia for over fifty thousand years. They once lived by gathering wild food and by hunting, and sometimes used boomerangs (left) to knock down their prey.

Australia is the smallest of the seven continents. The word Australia means "Southern Land." It was given this name by the Europeans, who first came here about 350 years ago.

Sydney is the largest city in Australia, with a population of over 3 million people. Its most famous building is the Opera House, built at the edge of its beautiful harbor. The roof of the Opera House looks like the sails of a ship.

For the capital cities of the smaller islands, look up the country name in the index.

MICR

PAPUA NEW GUINEA

ME

Port Moresby

ARAFURA SEA

TIMOR SEA

Darwin

CORAL SEA

GREAT DIVIDING RANGE

AUSTRALIA

INDIAN OCEAN

Perth

Darling River

Murray River

Brisba

Adelaide

Sydney

Canberra

Melbourne

TASMANIA

TASMA

kilometers
0   400   800   1200   1600

0   200   400   600   800   1000
miles

ARCTIC OCEAN

ATLANTIC OCEAN

INDIAN OCEAN

PACIFIC OCEAN

ARSHALL ISLANDS

DERATED
ATES OF
CRONESIA

Nauru is a tiny island which is just 8 square miles (21 sq km) in size. It is one of the smallest independent countries in the world.

The Polynesian islands lie in the middle of the South Pacific Ocean. Islanders used to travel vast distances between the islands in small sailing boats.

PACIFIC OCEAN

Equator

NAURU

KIRIBATI

SOLOMON ISLANDS

P O L Y N E S I A

■ Honiara

TUVALU

Tokelau (N.Z.)

Wallis and Futuna (France)

WESTERN SAMOA

American Samoa (U.S.A.)

Apia

VANUATU

Vila ■

Suva ■

TONGA

Cook Islands (N.Z.)

French Polynesia (France)

FIJI

Niue (N.Z.)

■ Nuku'alofa

ew Caledonia
(France)

New Zealand lies some 1,550 miles (2,500 km) rom Australia. It is made up of wo main islands. Most people ive on the North Island, where Auckland is the largest city.

Kermadec Islands (N.Z.)

North
Island

● Auckland

South
Island

■ Wellington

● Christchurch

N E W   Z E A L A N D

Chatham
Island (N.Z.)

Australia and the Pacific Islands

Australia is so big that it is called a continent. It is about the same size as the United States, without Alaska. The cities are all close to the coast. Inland, there are vast farms where sheep and cattle are raised, but most of central Australia is hot desert.

Like Australia, New Zealand is mainly English-speaking. Here the weather is mild, and snow falls on the mountains in winter. To the north is the Pacific Ocean, with thousands of warm, tropical islands. They include tiny islands, such as Nauru, which are among the smallest nations in the world.

31

ANSWER THAT!

1. What color is the famous swan of Western Australia?

2. What is the name of the rock in the center of Australia?

3. New Zealand has two birds, whose names begin with K, neither of which can fly. What are they?

Mount Wilhelm in Papua New Guinea is the highest mountain in the region, rising to 14,793 feet (4,509 m). Mount Cook, in New Zealand, is another high mountain, at 12,350 feet (3,764 m).

Crowned pigeon

Fruit bat

MOUNT WILHELM

Coconuts

Bird of parad

A R A F U R A   S E A

Crocodile

Taipan

Shrimp

C O R A L   S E A

T I M O R   S E A

GREAT BARRIER REEF

Grass tree

GREAT SANDY DESERT

AYERS ROCK

Kookaburra

I N D I A N   O C E A N

Frilled lizard

MacDONNELL RANGES

SIMPSON DESERT

Koala

Emu

GIBSON DESERT

GREAT VICTORIA DESERT

Wallaby

Lyrebird

Black swan

Darling River

Duck-billed platypus

Ring-tailed possum

Kangaroos are marsupials—animals that carry their young in a pouch.

Blue whale

Eucalyptus (gum) tree

The Darling River flows into the Murray River in Australia to form the longest river of the region. It is 2,330 miles (3,750 km) long.

Tasmanian devil

Shark

Sheep are important farm animals in both Australia and New Zealand. Some of the sheep and cattle stations (ranches) in Australia are as big as the country of Belgium. And there are about 18 times more sheep in New Zealand than there are people. Wool is sheared from the sheep to make cloth.

Anemone fish

Coconuts   Sweet lips

Giant clam

The Great Barrier Reef is the longest coral reef in the world. It stretches about 1,240 miles (2,000 km). The coral is made by tiny sea animals called polyps.

...tterfly fish   Coconuts

Kagu

Auger shell

Fairy tern

Tonna shell

Wandering albatross

Coconut palms are grown on many of the South Pacific islands.

PACIFIC   OCEAN

Wrasse

Tuna

Geysers gush up from the ground at Rotorua, New Zealand. They are like fountains of hot water. The water is heated by volcanic activity under the ground.

MAKING A MEAL OF IT
The warm weather of Australia is ideal for eating outdoors, and Australians love to have barbecues. They cook large steaks, as well as lamb, fish, and shrimp. For dessert they can have home-grown fruit, such as bananas, kiwifruit, pineapple, peaches, and watermelon.

Tuatara

ASMAN SEA

● Rotorua

Kakapo

Takahe

Shrimp

MOUNT COOK

Kiwi

33

A
B
C
D
E
F

ARCTIC OCEAN

PACIFIC OCEAN

ATLANTIC OCEAN

INDIAN OCEAN

The extent of the Arctic and Antarctic ice varies from summer to winter. This ice is known as pack ice.

Icebergs are huge blocks of ice that float in the seas close to Antarctica and the Arctic. Most of an iceberg is hidden beneath the water. Icebergs can be very dangerous to ships.

kilometers
0   200   400   600   800

0   100   200   300   400   500
miles

ANSWER THAT!

1. Which two kinds of seal are named after African animals?
2. Which biting insect lives around the Arctic?
3. One kind of bird can be seen in both Antarctica and the Arctic because it flies from one to the other. What is its name?

34

ATLANTIC OCEAN

The lowest temperature ever recorded comes from the Vostok research station in Antarctica: −128° Fahrenheit (−89°C). Antarctica is colder than the Arctic because the land takes longer to warm up in the summer sunlight.

The Vinson Massif is the highest mountain in Antarctica, rising to 16,863 feet (5,140 m). Mount Erebus is an active volcano.

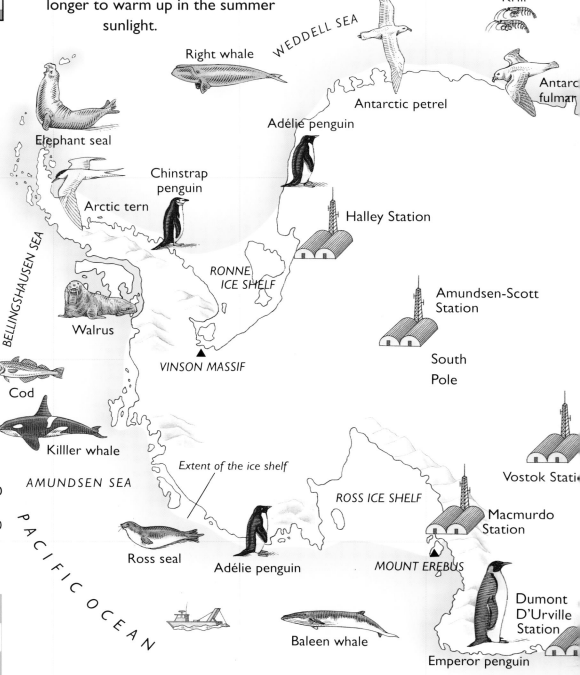

WEDDELL SEA

Krill

Right whale

Antarctic petrel

Adélie penguin

Antarctic fulmar

Elephant seal

Chinstrap penguin

Arctic tern

Halley Station

BELLINGSHAUSEN SEA

RONNE ICE SHELF

Amundsen-Scott Station

Walrus

South Pole

VINSON MASSIF

Cod

Killer whale

Extent of the ice shelf

Vostok Station

AMUNDSEN SEA

ROSS ICE SHELF

Macmurdo Station

PACIFIC OCEAN

Ross seal

Adélie penguin

MOUNT EREBUS

Dumont D'Urville Station

Baleen whale

Emperor penguin

Penguins are found only in the southern parts of the world, particularly around the edges of Antarctica. Emperor penguins are the largest kind. The males look after the eggs through the cold Antarctic winter and raise the young when they hatch.

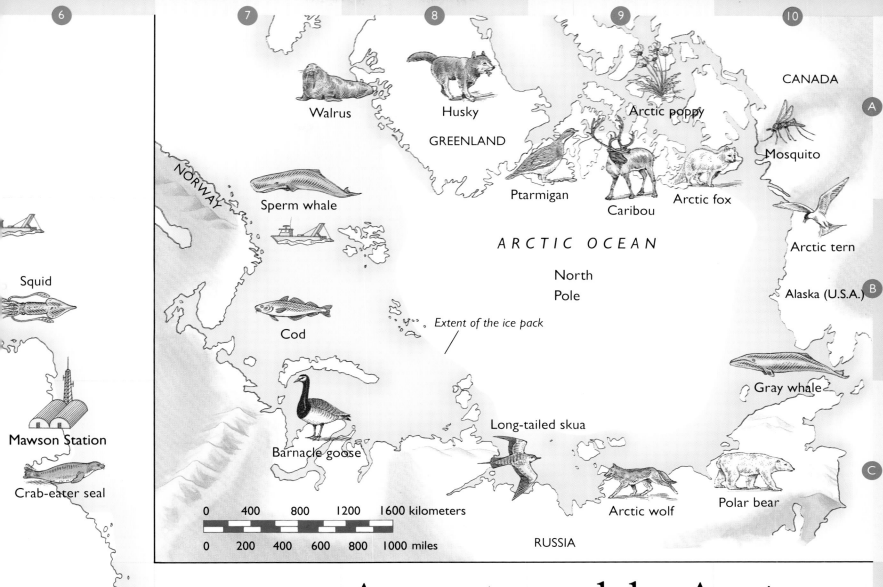

Walrus

Husky

GREENLAND

Arctic poppy

CANADA

Mosquito

NORWAY

Sperm whale

Ptarmigan

Caribou

Arctic fox

Arctic tern

ARCTIC OCEAN

North
Pole

Alaska (U.S.A.)

Squid

Cod

Extent of the ice pack

Gray whale

Mawson Station

Crab-eater seal

Barnacle goose

Long-tailed skua

Polar bear

0   400   800   1200   1600 kilometers

0   200   400   600   800   1000 miles

Arctic wolf

RUSSIA

INDIAN OCEAN

South Polar
skua

Casey Base

Leopard seal

Scientific stations carry
out research in various parts
of Antarctica, usually during
the short summer. The
scientists study such things
as weather patterns and
animal life.

Antarctica and the Arctic

The very top and bottom of the world
are the places that receive the least
sunlight, and in winter they get no
sunlight at all. These regions are bitterly
cold and covered with thick layers of ice and snow.
The farthest point south on our planet is called the
South Pole, and the farthest point north is called
the North Pole.

The South Pole is actually on land, in the middle
of the continent called Antarctica. The North
Pole is not on land at all, but on a huge sheet of ice
in the middle of the Arctic Ocean. The size of the
ice sheet changes as the ice melts and freezes
during the year. Neither Antarctica nor the
Arctic is owned by any country, and the only
people living there are explorers and scientists.

Flags of the World

North America

CANADA

UNITED STATES OF AMERICA

MEXICO

GUATEMALA

BELIZE

EL SALVADOR

HONDURAS

NICARAGUA

COSTA RICA

PANAMA

BAHAMAS

CUBA

JAMAICA

HAITI

DOMINICAN REPUBLIC

ANTIGUA AND BARBUDA

ST. KITTS AND NEVIS

DOMINICA

ST. LUCIA

BARBADOS

GRENADA

ST. VINCENT AND THE GRENADINES

TRINIDAD AND TOBAGO

South America

VENEZUELA

GUYANA

SURINAM

BRAZIL

COLOMBIA

ECUADOR

PERU

BOLIVIA

PARAGUAY

URUGUAY

CHILE

ARGENTINA

Europe

ICELAND

NORWAY

SWEDEN

FINLAND

DENMARK

IRELAND

UNITED KINGDOM

NETHERLANDS

BELGIUM

LUXEMBOURG

FRANCE

MONACO

SPAIN

ANDORRA

PORTUGAL

ITALY

SAN MARINO

VATICAN CITY STATE

MALTA

SWITZERLAND

LIECHTENSTEIN

AUSTRIA

GERMANY

POLAND

CZECH REPUBLIC

SLOVAKIA

HUNGARY

SLOVENIA

CROATIA

BOSNIA-HERZEGOVINA

YUGOSLAVIA

MACEDONIA

ALBANIA

GREECE

BULGARIA

ROMANIA

RUSSIA

ESTONIA

LATVIA

LITHUANIA

BELARUS

UKRAINE

MOLDOVA

Asia

GEORGIA

ARMENIA

AZERBAIJAN

KAZAKHSTAN

TURKMENISTAN

UZBEKISTAN

TAJIKISTAN

KYRGYZSTAN

TURKEY

CYPRUS

SYRIA

LEBANON

ISRAEL

JORDAN

SAUDI ARABIA

YEMEN

OMAN

UNITED ARAB EMIRATES

QATAR

BAHRAIN

KUWAIT

IRAQ

IRAN

AFGHANISTAN

PAKISTAN

INDIA

NEPAL

BHUTAN

BANGLADESH

SRI LANKA

MALDIVES

BURMA (MYANMAR)

THAILAND

CAMBODIA

LAOS

VIETNAM

CHINA

MONGOLIA

NORTH KOREA

SOUTH KOREA

JAPAN

TAIWAN

PHILIPPINES

BRUNEI

MALAYSIA

SINGAPORE

INDONESIA

Africa

MOROCCO

ALGERIA

TUNISIA

MAURITANIA

SENEGAL

GAMBIA

GUINEA-BISSAU

GUINEA

SIERRA LEONE

LIBERIA

COTE D'IVOIRE

MALI

BURKINA FASO

GHANA

TOGO

BENIN

NIGERIA

NIGER

CHAD

LIBYA

EGYPT

SUDAN

ERITREA

ETHIOPIA

DJIBOUTI

SOMALIA

KENYA

UGANDA

TANZANIA

BURUNDI

RWANDA

ZAIRE

CENTRAL AFRICAN REPUBLIC

CAMEROON

EQUATORIAL GUINEA

LESOTHO

MARSHALL ISLANDS

GABON

SWAZILAND

SOLOMON ISLANDS

SAO TOME AND PRINCIPE

MADAGASCAR

NAURU

CONGO

CAPE VERDE

TUVALU

ANGOLA

SEYCHELLES

KIRIBATI

ZAMBIA

COMOROS

VANUATU

MALAWI

MAURITIUS

FIJI

MOZAMBIQUE

Australia and the Pacific

TONGA

ZIMBABWE

PAPUA NEW GUINEA

WESTERN SAMOA

BOTSWANA

AUSTRALIA

NAMIBIA

NEW ZEALAND

SOUTH AFRICA

FEDERATED STATES OF MICRONESIA

38

Index

Legend:
- National capitals ■
- State and provincial capitals ★
- Important cities ●
- State and provincial capitals
- State and provincial borders
- National borders

0 125 250 375 500 625 miles

0 250 500 750 1000 kilometers

Banff National Park contains spectacular scenery of lakes and mountains. It is one of many national parks in Canada and the United States which have been set up to protect the landscape and wildlife.

Oil has been discovered in large quantities in northern Alaska. A pipeline carries the oil 780 miles (1,250 km) to the south coast. Alaska's oil fields are twice as large as any other oil fields in North America.

Hockey is national sp Canada. It and excitin played on s rinks by tw six players. only major players to b play is in pr was first pla about 120 y

Mount Rushmore, in South Dakota, is the site of four huge portraits of American presidents. They were carved out of the rockface between 1927 and 1941 by the sculptor Gutzon Borglum. The four presidents are George Washington, Thomas Jefferson, Theodore Roosevelt, and Abraham Lincoln.

BERING STRAIT

ARCTIC OCE

ALASKA

Victoria Is

▲ MOUNT McKINLEY

● Anchorage

Yukon River

Mackenzie River

Great Bear Lake

YUKON

NORTHWEST TERR

★ Whitehorse

Juneau ★

★ Yellowknife

Great Slave Lake

BRITISH UMBIA

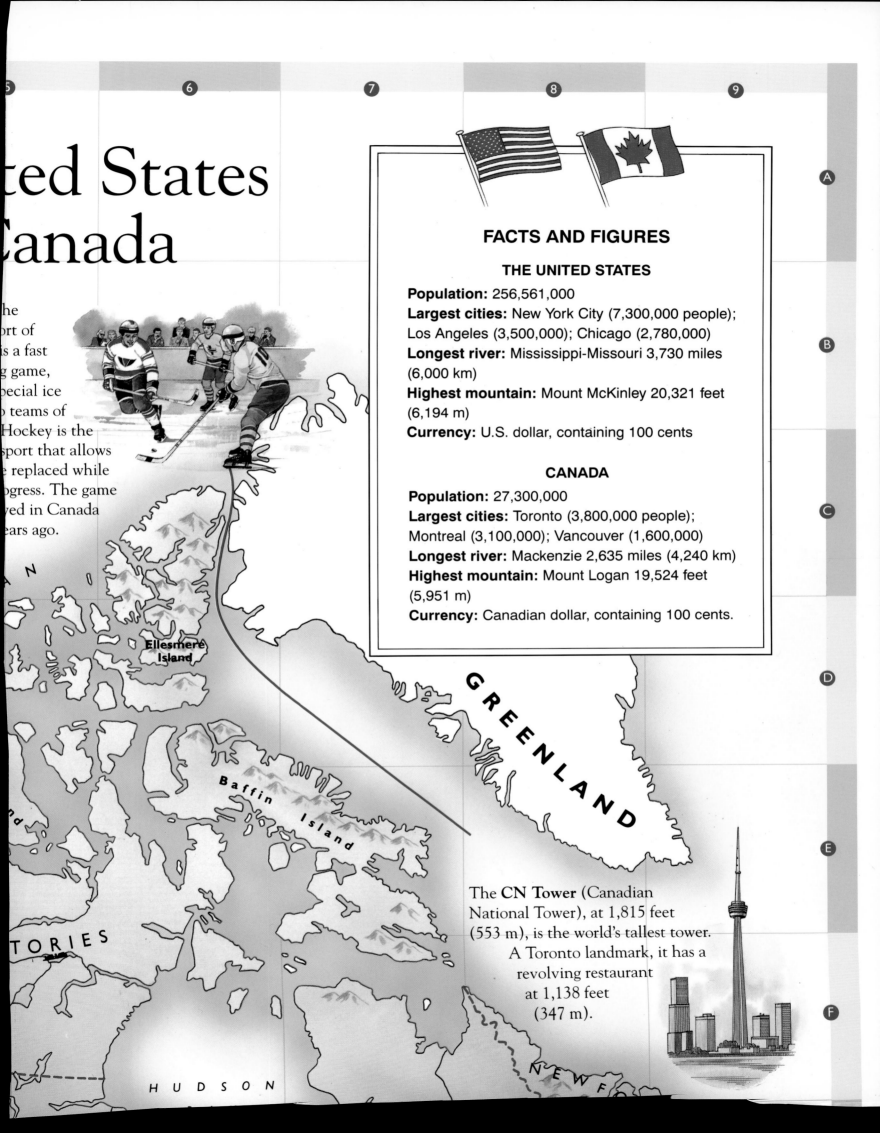

ted States
anada

he
rt of
s a fast
game,
pecial ice
teams of
Hockey is the
sport that allows
replaced while
gress. The game
ved in Canada
ears ago.

Ellesmere Island

Baffin Island

TORIES

HUDSON

GREENLAND

FACTS AND FIGURES

THE UNITED STATES

Population: 256,561,000
Largest cities: New York City (7,300,000 people); Los Angeles (3,500,000); Chicago (2,780,000)
Longest river: Mississippi-Missouri 3,730 miles (6,000 km)
Highest mountain: Mount McKinley 20,321 feet (6,194 m)
Currency: U.S. dollar, containing 100 cents

CANADA

Population: 27,300,000
Largest cities: Toronto (3,800,000 people); Montreal (3,100,000); Vancouver (1,600,000)
Longest river: Mackenzie 2,635 miles (4,240 km)
Highest mountain: Mount Logan 19,524 feet (5,951 m)
Currency: Canadian dollar, containing 100 cents.

The **CN Tower** (Canadian National Tower), at 1,815 feet (553 m), is the world's tallest tower. A Toronto landmark, it has a revolving restaurant at 1,138 feet (347 m).

NEWF

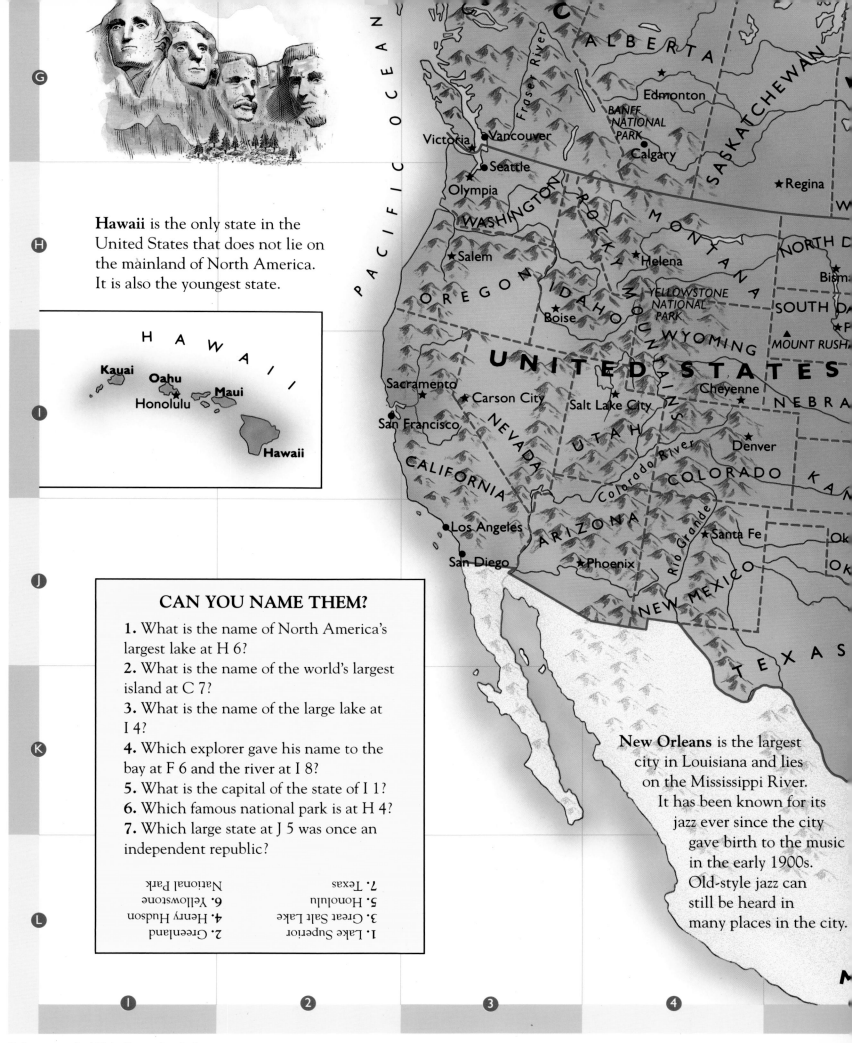

Hawaii is the only state in the United States that does not lie on the mainland of North America. It is also the youngest state.

H A W A I I

Kauai
Oahu
Honolulu
Maui
Hawaii

PACIFIC OCEAN

ALBERTA
SASKATCHEWAN
Edmonton
BANFF NATIONAL PARK
Victoria · Vancouver
Calgary
★ Regina
Seattle
Olympia
WASHINGTON
ROCKY
MONTANA
NORTH D
Bism
Salem
Helena
IDAHO
YELLOWSTONE NATIONAL PARK
SOUTH DA
OREGON
Boise
WYOMING
P
MOUNT RUSH
U N I T E D   S T A T E S
Sacramento
Carson City
Salt Lake City
Cheyenne
NEBRA
San Francisco
NEVADA
UTAH
Colorado River
Denver
COLORADO
KAN
CALIFORNIA
Los Angeles
ARIZONA
Rio Grande
Santa Fe
Ok
San Diego
Phoenix
NEW MEXICO
OK
TEXAS
M

CAN YOU NAME THEM?

1. What is the name of North America's largest lake at H 6?

2. What is the name of the world's largest island at C 7?

3. What is the name of the large lake at I 4?

4. Which explorer gave his name to the bay at F 6 and the river at I 8?

5. What is the capital of the state of I 1?

6. Which famous national park is at H 4?

7. Which large state at J 5 was once an independent republic?

1. Lake Superior   5. Honolulu
2. Greenland   6. Yellowstone National Park
3. Great Salt Lake   7. Texas
4. Henry Hudson

New Orleans is the largest city in Louisiana and lies on the Mississippi River. It has been known for its jazz ever since the city gave birth to the music in the early 1900s. Old-style jazz can still be heard in many places in the city.

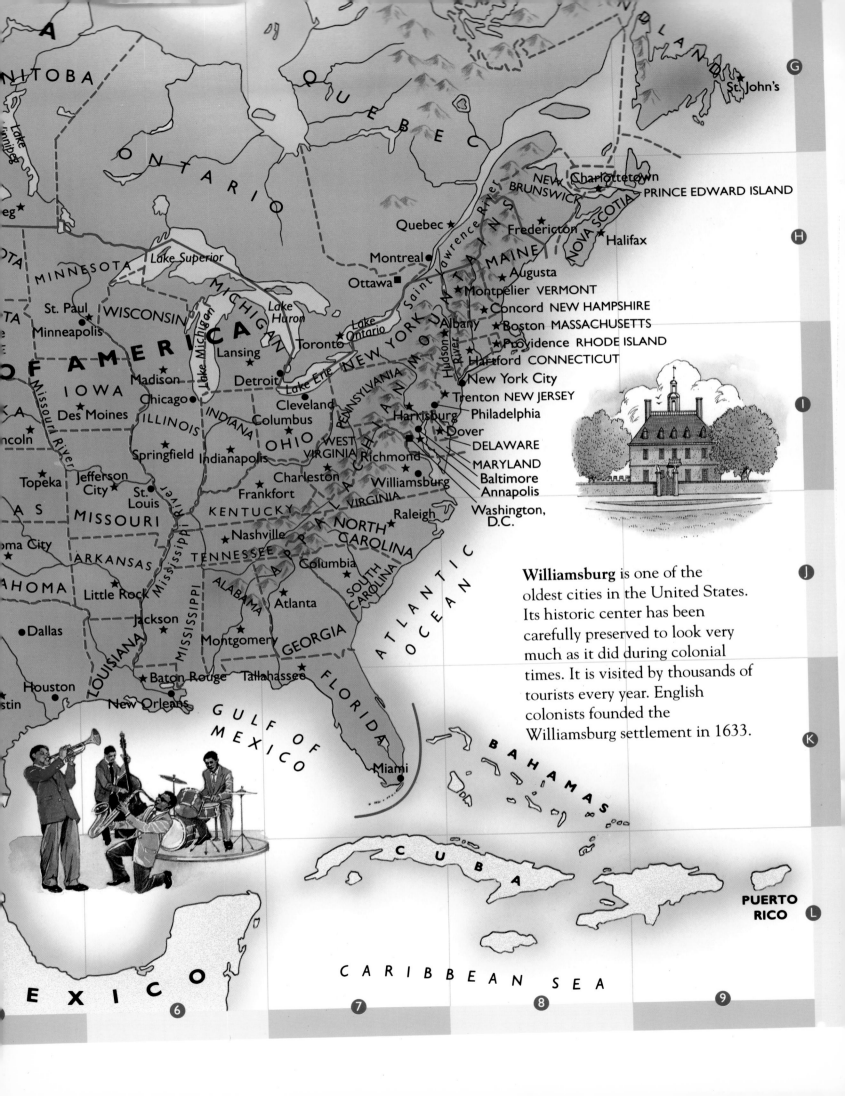

St. John's

G

NEW BRUNSWICK
Charlottetown
PRINCE EDWARD ISLAND

Quebec
Fredericton
Halifax
NOVA SCOTIA

H

Montreal
Ottawa

Saint Lawrence River

MAINE

Augusta
Montpelier VERMONT
Concord NEW HAMPSHIRE
Albany Boston MASSACHUSETTS
Providence RHODE ISLAND
Hartford CONNECTICUT
New York City
Trenton NEW JERSEY
Harrisburg Philadelphia
Dover
DELAWARE
MARYLAND
Baltimore
Annapolis
Washington, D.C.

Hudson River

NEW YORK

MINNESOTA
Lake Superior
St. Paul WISCONSIN
Minneapolis
Lake Huron
MICHIGAN
Lake Michigan
Madison
Lansing
Toronto
Lake Ontario
Lake Erie
Detroit
IOWA
Des Moines
Chicago
Cleveland
INDIANA
Columbus
ILLINOIS
OHIO
Springfield
Indianapolis
WEST VIRGINIA
Richmond
Williamsburg
VIRGINIA
Charleston
Frankfort
KENTUCKY
Topeka
Jefferson City
St. Louis
Lincoln
Missouri River
Mississippi River

OF AMERICA

ONTARIO

QUEBEC

MANITOBA

I

APPALACHIAN MOUNTAINS

Raleigh
NORTH CAROLINA

MISSOURI
Nashville
TENNESSEE
ARKANSAS
Columbia
SOUTH CAROLINA

J

Williamsburg is one of the oldest cities in the United States. Its historic center has been carefully preserved to look very much as it did during colonial times. It is visited by thousands of tourists every year. English colonists founded the Williamsburg settlement in 1633.

oma City
Little Rock
AHOMA
Jackson
Dallas
MISSISSIPPI
ALABAMA
Atlanta
Montgomery
GEORGIA
LOUISIANA
Baton Rouge
Tallahassee
Houston
New Orleans

ATLANTIC OCEAN

GULF OF MEXICO

FLORIDA

Miami

K

BAHAMAS

MEXICO

CUBA

PUERTO RICO

L

CARIBBEAN SEA

6   7   8   9